To:

*In all things God works
for the good of those who love him,
who have been called
according to his purpose.*

ROMANS 8:28 NIV

From:

ZONDERVAN BOOKS

The Purpose Driven Life: Selected Thoughts and Scriptures for the Graduate
Copyright © 2013 by Rick Warren

Requests for information should be addressed to:
Zondervan, *3900 Sparks Dr. SE, Grand Rapids, Michigan 49546*

Zondervan titles may be purchased in bulk for educational, business, fundraising, or sales promotional use. For information, please email SpecialMarkets@ Zondervan.com.

ISBN 978-0-310-36512-9 (hardcover)

The Scripture versions cited in this book are identified in the sources page, which hereby becomes a part of this copyright page.

Cover design: Jorden Collins
Interior design: Jorden Collins
Interior photos: iStock

Printed in Malaysia

21 22 23 24 25 /IMG/ 10 9 8 7 6 5 4 3 2 1

RICK WARREN

THE PURPOSE DRIVEN LIFE

SELECTED THOUGHTS
& SCRIPTURES *for the*
GRADUATE
updated edition

ZONDERVAN BOOKS

Dear Graduate,

Congratulations! You made it. The papers are finished, the tests have been taken, and you are now a graduate. You're closing the chapter on one part of your life and beginning to write a new one. You're excited and hopeful, scared and unsure, all at the same time. Perhaps you're asking, "Where do I go from here? What is my purpose in life?"

In this book, made especially for you, you'll discover that no matter who you are or where you live, God has five special purposes for your life. As you seek to fulfill them, everything else will fall into place.

God has great and wonderful plans for you. So, sit back, relax, and let him speak to your soul as you read. May God open your eyes so that you can see your unique purpose in this life.

WHAT ON EARTH AM I HERE FOR?

"Why do I exist?"

"Why am I here?"

"What is my purpose?"

These are the most fundamental questions you can ask in life. Have you ever asked these questions, wondering where to turn for the answer?

Contrary to what many popular books, movies, and seminars tell you, you won't discover your life's meaning by looking within yourself. You didn't create yourself, so there is no way you can tell yourself what you were created for! You must begin with God, your Creator.

It is God who directs the lives of his creatures;
everyone's life is in his power.
JOB 12:10 GNT

IT IS ONLY IN GOD THAT WE DISCOVER OUR ORIGIN, OUR IDENTITY, OUR MEANING, OUR PURPOSE, OUR SIGNIFICANCE, AND OUR DESTINY.

You know me inside and out,
you know every bone in my body;
You know exactly how I was made, bit by bit,
how I was sculpted from nothing into something.

PSALM 139:15 The Message

IT ALL STARTS WITH GOD

The exciting truth is that God has never created anything without a purpose. Colossians 1:16 says: *"For everything, absolutely everything, above and below, visible and invisible, . . . everything got started in him and finds its purpose in him"* (The Message). The very fact that you're alive means God has a purpose for your life!

And you weren't created for just one purpose. You were created for five special reasons that are explained in God's Word. As you start this new chapter in your life, may you come to understand God's wonderful plan for you and find answers to life's most important questions.

It's in Christ that we find out who we are and what we are living for. Long before we first heard of Christ and got our hopes up, he had his eye on us, had designs on us for glorious living, part of the overall purpose he is working out in everything and everyone.

EPHESIANS 1:11–12 The Message

YOU WERE PLANNED
FOR GOD'S PLEASURE!

*You are worthy, O Lord our God, to receive glory
and honor and power. For you created all things.*

REVELATION 4:11 NLT

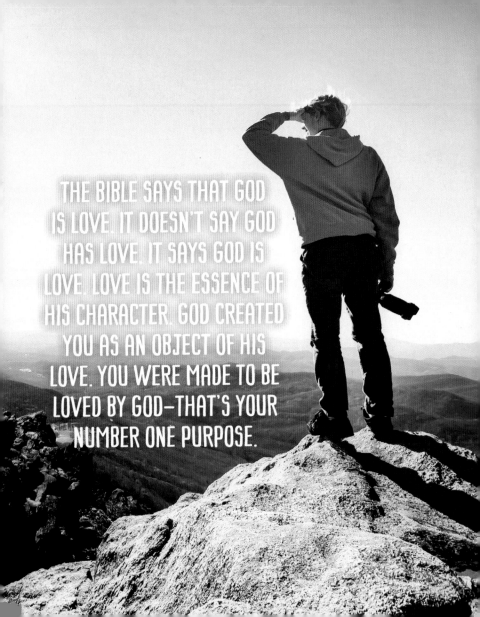

THE BIBLE SAYS THAT GOD IS LOVE. IT DOESN'T SAY GOD HAS LOVE. IT SAYS GOD IS LOVE. LOVE IS THE ESSENCE OF HIS CHARACTER. GOD CREATED YOU AS AN OBJECT OF HIS LOVE. YOU WERE MADE TO BE LOVED BY GOD—THAT'S YOUR NUMBER ONE PURPOSE.

Long before he laid down earth's foundations, [God] had us in mind, had settled on us as the focus of his love, to be made whole and holy by his love.

EPHESIANS 1:4 The Message

Because of his love God had already decided that through Jesus Christ he would make us his children— this was his pleasure and purpose.

EPHESIANS 1:4–5 GNT

///

We know and rely on the love God has for us. God is love. Whoever lives in love lives in God, and God in them.

1 JOHN 4:16 NIV

///

The only accurate way to understand ourselves is by what God is and by what he does for us.

ROMANS 12:3 The Message

No mere man has ever seen, heard, or even imagined what wonderful things God has ready for those who love the Lord.

1 CORINTHIANS 2:9 TLB

The LORD be exalted, who delights in the well-being of his servant.

PSALM 35:27 NIV

*As a father has compassion on his children, so the
LORD has compassion on those who fear him.*
PSALM 103:13 NIV

GOD DIDN'T NEED TO LOVE YOU. HE WASN'T LONELY. HE DIDN'T NEED SERVANTS. HE WASN'T BORED. GOD CREATED HUMANS BECAUSE HE WANTED TO LOVE US. WE WERE PLANNED FOR HIS PLEASURE.

The LORD takes pleasure in His people.
PSALM 149:4 NASB

*Smile on me, your servant;
teach me the right way to live.*
PSALM 119:135 The Message

*The LORD directs the steps of the godly.
He delights in every detail of their lives.*
PSALM 37:23 NLT

*God's wisdom is something mysterious that goes deep into the
interior of his purposes. You don't find it lying around on the
surface. It's not the latest message, but more like the oldest—
what God determined as the way to bring out his best in us,
long before we ever arrived on the scene.*
1 CORINTHIANS 2:7 The Message

May the glory of the LORD endure forever;
may the LORD rejoice in his works.

PSALM 104:31 NIV

//

[God] takes pleasure in those who honor him; in those who trust in his constant love.

PSALM 147:11 GNT

//

[The LORD] brought me out into a spacious place;
he rescued me because he delighted in me.

PSALM 18:19 NIV

The steps of a man are established by the LORD,
when he delights in his way.

PSALM 37:23 ESV

God created mankind in his own image,
in the image of God he created them;
male and female he created them.

GENESIS 1:27 NIV

The God who made the world and everything in it
is the Lord of heaven and earth. . . . And he is not
served by human hands, as if he needed anything.
Rather, he himself gives everyone life and breath
and everything else. From one man he made all the
nations, that they should inhabit the whole earth; and
he marked out their appointed times in history and
the boundaries of their lands. God did this so that
they would seek him and perhaps reach out for him
and find him, though he is not far from any one of us.

ACTS 17:24–27 NIV

I am your Creator. You were in my care
even before you were born.

ISAIAH 44:2 CEV

GOD MADE US IN HIS IMAGE. THAT MEANS WE ARE UNLIKE ANYTHING ELSE IN ALL OF CREATION. WE ALONE WERE GIVEN THE CAPACITY TO KNOW GOD AND TO LOVE HIM AND TO HAVE HIM KNOW AND LOVE US IN RETURN.

MADE TO LAST FOREVER

Right now, you're probably thinking only about your immediate future—college, your career, or maybe even marriage. And while those things are important, there is also another life waiting for you after this one. God designed you, in his image, to live for eternity.

This world is fading away, along with everything that people crave. But anyone who does what pleases God will live forever.

1 JOHN 2:17 NLT

When this tent we live in—our body here on earth— is torn down, God will have a house in heaven for us to live in, a home he himself has made, which will last forever.

2 CORINTHIANS 5:1 GNT

I am here on earth for just a little while.

PSALM 119:19 GNT

This world is not our home; we are looking forward to our everlasting home in heaven.

HEBREWS 13:14 TLB

There are many whose conduct shows they are really enemies of the cross of Christ. . . . they think only about this life here on earth. But we are citizens of heaven, where the Lord Jesus Christ lives.

PHILIPPIANS 3:18–20 NLT

We fix our eyes not on what is seen, but on what is unseen, since what is seen is temporary, but what is unseen is eternal.

2 CORINTHIANS 4:18 NIV

Every moment we spend in these earthly bodies is time spent away from our eternal home in heaven with Jesus.

2 CORINTHIANS 5:6 TLB

Friends, this world is not your home, so don't make yourselves cozy in it. Don't indulge your ego at the expense of your soul.

1 PETER 2:11 The Message

All these [heroes of the faith] died in faith. They did not get the things that God promised his people, but they saw them coming far in the future and were glad. They said they were like visitors and strangers on earth. . . . They were waiting for a better country—a heavenly country. So God is not ashamed to be called their God, because he has prepared a city for them.

HEBREWS 11:13, 16 NCV

The things we see now are here today, gone tomorrow. But the things we can't see now will last forever.

2 CORINTHIANS 4:18 The Message

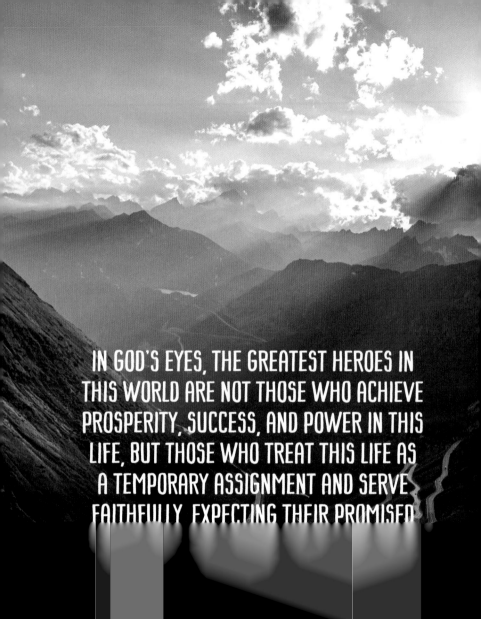

IN GOD'S EYES, THE GREATEST HEROES IN THIS WORLD ARE NOT THOSE WHO ACHIEVE PROSPERITY, SUCCESS, AND POWER IN THIS LIFE, BUT THOSE WHO TREAT THIS LIFE AS A TEMPORARY ASSIGNMENT AND SERVE FAITHFULLY, EXPECTING THEIR PROMISED

I have loved you with an everlasting love;
I have drawn you with unfailing kindness.

JEREMIAH 31:3 NIV

You saw me before I was born and scheduled
each day of my life before I began to breathe.
Every day was recorded in your book!

PSALM 139:16 TLB

God decided to give us life through the word
of truth so we might be the most important
of all the things he made.

JAMES 1:18 NCV

I have carried you since you were born;
I have taken care of you from your birth.
Even when you are old, I will be the same.
Even when your hair has turned gray, I will take
care of you. I made you and will take care of you.

ISAIAH 46:3–4 NCV

THE FIRST PURPOSE FOR YOUR LIFE IS TO KNOW AND TO LOVE GOD BECAUSE THAT GIVES GOD PLEASURE. THE MOST IMPORTANT THING YOU CAN KNOW IN LIFE IS THAT GOD LOVES YOU.

THE MOST IMPORTANT THING YOU CAN
DO IN LIFE IS LOVE HIM BACK.

GOD KNOWS EVERYTHING ABOUT YOU
AND HE LOVES YOU. HIS DEEPEST DESIRE
IS FOR YOU TO KNOW HIM AND LOVE
HIM IN RETURN.

*Worthy are you, our Lord and God,
to receive glory and honor and power,
for you created all things.*

REVELATION 4:11 ESV

///

Jesus replied, "Love the Lord your God
with all your heart and with all your soul
and with all your mind. This is the first
and greatest commandment."

MATTHEW 22:37–38 NIV

///

The LORD is pleased with only those who worship
him and trust his love.

PSALM 147:11 CEV

I will thank the LORD at all times.
My mouth will always praise him.

PSALM 34:1 GW

Take your everyday, ordinary life—your sleeping,
eating, going-to-work, and walking-around life—
and place it before God as an offering.

ROMANS 12:1 The Message

I don't want your sacrifices—I want your love; I don't
want your offerings—I want you to know me.

HOSEA 6:6 TLB

Figure out what will please Christ, and then do it.

EPHESIANS 5:10 The Message

SO, INSTEAD OF TRYING TO DO AND SAY ALL THE RIGHT THINGS TO MAKE GOD LOVE YOU, ALL YOU HAVE TO DO IS REALIZE HE LOVES YOU ALREADY, AND LOVE HIM BACK.

*If you love me, you will
obey my commandments.*

JOHN 14:15 GNT

*By [Christ] therefore let us offer the sacrifice
of praise to God continually, that is, the fruit
of our lips giving thanks to his name.*

HEBREWS 13:15 KJV

*I will praise God's name in song
and glorify him with thanksgiving.
This will please the LORD.*

PSALM 69:30–31 NIV

*Well-formed love banishes fear. Since fear is crippling,
a fearful life—fear of death, fear of judgment—
is not one yet fully formed in love.*

1 JOHN 4:18 The Message

You, LORD, give perfect peace to those who keep their
purpose firm and put their trust in you.

ISAIAH 26:3 GNT

I focus on this one thing: Forgetting the past
and looking forward to what lies ahead,
I press on to reach the end of the race and
receive the heavenly prize for which God,
through Christ Jesus, is calling us.

PHILIPPIANS 3:13–14 NLT

Let's keep focused on that goal, those of us who
want everything God has for us. If any of you have
something else in mind, something less than total
commitment, God will clear your blurred vision—
you'll see it yet!

PHILIPPIANS 3:15 The Message

GOD WILL EVEN HELP YOU TO KNOW HIM MORE. ALL YOU NEED TO DO IS ASK, PERHAPS WITH A PRAYER LIKE THIS:

"God, if I don't get anything else done today, help me to know you a little bit better and love you a little bit more. If, at the end of the day, I know you a little bit better and I love you a little bit more, I have not wasted this day. If I loved you and knew you a little bit more, I just fulfilled the first purpose of my life."

WHAT DRIVES YOUR LIFE?

Perhaps you've been trying to find your purpose in life through a career, your education, or a relationship. These things alone, no matter how wonderful and fulfilling, are not your purpose. If you are searching for your purpose in life, don't worry about seeking out your gifts and talents, your goals or visions; start with your first and most important purpose—loving and knowing God. Everything else will fall into place when you seek first to fulfill this purpose for your life.

Why do you worry about clothes? See how the flowers of the field grow. They do not labor or spin. Yet I tell you that not even Solomon in all his splendor was dressed like one of these. If that is how God clothes the grass of the field, which is here today and tomorrow is thrown into the fire, will he not much more clothe you? . . . So do not worry, saying, "What shall we eat?" or "What shall we drink?" or "What shall we wear?" For . . . your heavenly Father knows that you need them. But seek first his kingdom and his righteousness, and all these things will be given to you as well.

MATTHEW 6:28–33 NIV

WHAT MAKES GOD SMILE?

When you love God, you want to express it. That is called worship. Whether you're singing a song or praying, or simply enjoying a beautiful sunset and thanking God in your heart, that is worship.

[God's] pleasure is not in the strength of the horse, nor his delight in the legs of a warrior; the LORD delights in those who fear him, who put their hope in his unfailing love.

PSALM 147:10–11 NIV

Come, let us bow down in worship, let us kneel before the LORD our Maker; for he is our God and we are the people of his pasture, the flock under his care.

PSALM 95:6–7 NIV

That's the kind of people the Father is out looking for: those who are simply and honestly themselves before him in their worship.

JOHN 4:23 The Message

WORSHIP IS SIMPLY ANYTHING THAT GIVES GOD PLEASURE. AND WORSHIP IS THE FIRST PURPOSE OF YOUR LIFE!

*Use your whole body as an instrument
to do what is right for the glory of God.*

ROMANS 6:13 NLT

*As I have loved you, so you must love one another.
By this everyone will know that you are
my disciples, if you love one another.*

JOHN 13:34–35 NIV

*Offer your bodies as a living sacrifice,
holy and pleasing to God—this is your
true and proper worship.*

ROMANS 12:1 NIV

*May you always be filled with the fruit of your
salvation—the righteous character produced
in your life by Jesus Christ—for this will bring
much glory and praise to God.*

PHILIPPIANS 1:11 NLT

*God has given each of you a gift from his great variety
of spiritual gifts. Use them well to serve one another. . . .
Do you have the gift of helping others? Do it with all the
strength and energy that God supplies. Then everything
you do will bring glory to God.*

1 PETER 4:10–11 NLT

*As God's grace reaches more and more people . . .
God will receive more and more glory.*

2 CORINTHIANS 4:15 NLT

*Whatever you do, work at it with all your heart,
as working for the Lord, not for human masters.*

COLOSSIANS 3:23 NIV

*Just tell me what to do and I will do it, Lord.
As long as I live I'll wholeheartedly obey.*

PSALM 119:33 TLB

YOU WERE FORMED
FOR A FAMILY!

*God decided in advance to adopt us into his own family
by bringing us to himself through Jesus Christ. This is
what he wanted to do, and it gave him great pleasure.*

EPHESIANS 1:5 NLT

From the beginning of time, God has always wanted a family. He wants you to be a part of that family—a family that will last for all eternity.

Hebrews 2:11 is an amazing verse:

Jesus and the people He makes holy all belong to the same family. That's why He isn't ashamed to call them His brothers and sisters. (NJB)

Jesus Christ calls us his brothers and sisters! We're not just called to believe. We're called to belong—to belong to the family of God.

See how very much our heavenly Father loves us, for he calls us his children, and that is what we are!

1 JOHN 3:1 NLT

[Jesus] pointed to his disciples and said, "Look, these are my mother and brothers. Anyone who does the will of my Father in heaven is my brother and sister and mother!"

MATTHEW 12:49–50 NLT

God is the One who made all things, and all things are for his glory. He wanted to have many children share his glory.

HEBREWS 2:10 NCV

It is his boundless mercy that has given us the privilege of being born again, so that we are now members of God's own family.

1 PETER 1:3 TLB

You are all children of God through faith in Christ Jesus.

GALATIANS 3:26 NLT

It was a happy day for [God] when he gave us our new lives through the truth of his Word, and we became, as it were, the first children in his new family.

JAMES 1:18 TLB

The moment you were spiritually born into God's family, you were given some astounding birthday gifts: the family name, the family likeness, family privileges, family intimate access, and the family inheritance!

You may know the hope to which he
has called you, the riches of his
glorious inheritance in his holy people.

EPHESIANS 1:18 NIV

//

Since you are his child, God will give you
all that he has for his children.

GALATIANS 4:7 GNT

//

My God will meet all your needs according to
the riches of his glory in Christ Jesus.

PHILIPPIANS 4:19 NIV

And we have a priceless inheritance—an inheritance
that is kept in heaven for you, pure and undefiled,
beyond the reach of change and decay.

1 PETER 1:4 NLT

WHAT DOES THE FAMILY OF GOD LOOK LIKE? WHERE CAN IT BE FOUND?

God has given us the privilege of being born again so that now we are members of God's own family. That family is the church of the living God, the support and foundation of the truth.

1 PETER 1:3 NJB

Some of us are Jews, some are Gentiles, some are slaves, and some are free. But we have all been baptized into one body by one Spirit, and we all share the same Spirit.

1 CORINTHIANS 12:13 NLT

God's family is the church of the living God, the pillar and foundation of the truth.

1 TIMOTHY 3:15 GW

What happens when a building has no support and foundation? It collapses. In just the same way, you need support from other people and a foundation to keep you strong in your walk with God. You find that loving support when you join your brothers and sisters in Christ's church—the family of God.

As you make your way in the "real world," it will be important to establish yourself on a solid foundation—surround yourself with Christian friends and mentors, and make attending church a priority. As a family, we all need each other!

In [Christ] the whole building is joined together and rises to become a holy temple in the Lord. And in him you too are being built together to become a dwelling in which God lives by his Spirit.

EPHESIANS 2:21–22 NIV

Each part gets its meaning from the body as a whole, not the other way around. The body we're talking about is Christ's body of chosen people. Each of us finds our meaning and function as a part of his body. But as a chopped-off finger or cut-off toe we wouldn't amount to much, would we?

ROMANS 12:4–5 The Message

From [Christ] the whole body, joined and held
together by every supporting ligament, grows and
builds itself up in love, as each part does its work.

EPHESIANS 4:16 NIV

The way God designed our bodies is
a model for understanding our lives
together as a church: every part
dependent on every other part.

1 CORINTHIANS 12:25 The Message

Just as a body, though one, has many parts, but all its many
parts form one body, so it is with Christ. For we were all baptized
by one Spirit so as to form one body—whether Jews or Gentiles,
slave or free—and we were all given the one Spirit to drink. Even
so the body is not made up of one part but of many. Now if the
foot should say, "Because I am not a hand, I do not belong to the
body," it would not for that reason stop being part of the body.
And if the ear should say, "Because I am not an eye, I do not
belong to the body," it would not for that reason cease to be part
of the body. If the whole body were an eye, where would the sense
of hearing be? If the whole body were an ear, where would the
sense of smell be? But in fact God has arranged the parts in the
body, every one of them, just as he wanted them to be.

1 CORINTHIANS 12:12–18 NIV

*Just as each of us has one body
with many members, and these members
do not all have the same function,
so in Christ we who are many form
one body, and each member
belongs to all the others.*

ROMANS 12:4–5 NIV

THE CHURCH IS A BODY, NOT A BUSINESS;
A FAMILY, NOT AN INSTITUTION. GOD SAYS,
"I FORMED YOU TO BE A PART OF MY FAMILY."
WHEN YOU BECOME PART OF THE FAMILY OF
GOD, YOU ARE SO CLOSE THAT YOU ARE ALL
ACTUALLY PART OF THE SAME BODY.

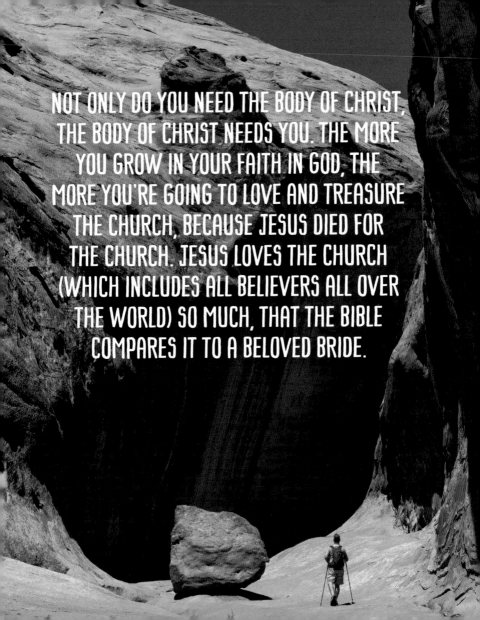

NOT ONLY DO YOU NEED THE BODY OF CHRIST, THE BODY OF CHRIST NEEDS YOU. THE MORE YOU GROW IN YOUR FAITH IN GOD, THE MORE YOU'RE GOING TO LOVE AND TREASURE THE CHURCH, BECAUSE JESUS DIED FOR THE CHURCH. JESUS LOVES THE CHURCH (WHICH INCLUDES ALL BELIEVERS ALL OVER THE WORLD) SO MUCH, THAT THE BIBLE COMPARES IT TO A BELOVED BRIDE.

To one person the Spirit gives the ability to give wise advice; to another the same Spirit gives a message of special knowledge. The same Spirit gives great faith to another, and to someone else the one Spirit gives the gift of healing. He gives one person the power to perform miracles, and to another the ability to prophesy. He gives someone else the ability to discern whether a message is from the Spirit of God or from another spirit. Still another person is given the ability to speak in unknown languages, while another is given the ability to interpret what is being said. It is the one and only Holy Spirit who distributes all these gifts. He alone decides which gift each person should have.

1 CORINTHIANS 12:8–11 NLT

Christ loved the church and gave himself up for her to make her holy, cleansing her by the washing with water through the word, and to present her to himself as a radiant church, without stain or wrinkle or any other blemish, but holy and blameless.

EPHESIANS 5:25–27 NIV

As a bridegroom rejoices over his bride, so will your God rejoice over you.

ISAIAH 62:5 NIV

[God] creates each of us by Christ Jesus to join him in the work he does, the good work he has gotten ready for us to do, work we had better be doing.

EPHESIANS 2:10 The Message

JUST LIKE IN AN EARTHLY FAMILY, WHERE YOU RECEIVE LOVE, BUT ALSO GIVE IT, IN GOD'S FAMILY, WE ARE CALLED TO LOVE AND CARE FOR OUR FELLOW MEMBERS.

THERE ARE 58 "ONE ANOTHERS" IN THE BIBLE THAT TEACH US HOW TO TREAT OUR BROTHERS AND SISTERS IN THE FAMILY OF GOD. THEY INCLUDE:

Love one another

*Dear friends, since God so loved us,
we also ought to love one another.*

1 JOHN 4:11 NIV

*Love means living the way God commanded us to live.
As you have heard from the beginning, his command
is this: Live a life of love.*

2 JOHN 1:6 NCV

Show special love for God's people.

1 PETER 2:17 CEV

*[Jesus said,] "Your strong love for each other
will prove to the world that you are my disciples."*

JOHN 13:35 TLB

Encourage one another

*Let us not give up the habit of meeting together,
as some are doing. Instead, let us encourage one another.*

HEBREWS 10:25 GNT

*Encourage one another daily . . . so that none
of you may be hardened by sin's deceitfulness.*

HEBREWS 3:13 NIV

*If you know people who have wandered off
from God's truth, don't write them off.
Go after them. Get them back.*

JAMES 5:19 The Message

Pray for one another

*You should be like one big happy family, full of
sympathy toward each other, loving one another
with tender hearts and humble minds.*

1 PETER 3:8 TLB

*Confess your sins to each other
and pray for each other.*

JAMES 5:16 NIV

Serve one another

Serve one another humbly in love.
GALATIANS 5:13 NIV

I want us to help each other with the faith we have. Your faith will help me, and my faith will help you.
ROMANS 1:12 NCV

As each part does its own special work, it helps the other parts grow, so that the whole body is healthy and growing and full of love.
EPHESIANS 4:16 NLT

Jesus Christ laid down his life for us. And we ought to lay down our lives for our brothers and sisters.
1 JOHN 3:16 NIV

Whenever you possibly can, do good to those who need it. Never tell your neighbors to wait until tomorrow if you can help them now.
PROVERBS 3:27–28 GNT

WHEN YOU PARTICIPATE IN GOD'S FAMILY, BY LOVING AND CARING FOR EACH OTHER, THAT'S CALLED *FELLOWSHIP*. FELLOWSHIP IS THE SECOND PURPOSE OF YOUR LIFE.

Real fellowship means being as committed to each other as we are to Jesus. First John 3:16 says:

We understand what real love is when we realize that Christ gave His life for us. That means that we must give our lives for other believers. (NJB)

Giving yourself, putting others first, isn't easy, but God asks you to do it only because he did it first. He loves us, even though we aren't perfect, and his purpose for you is to do the same. Jesus wants you to love real people, not ideal people—because, after all, no one is ideal.

If we walk in the light, as [God] is in the light, we have fellowship with one another, and the blood of Jesus, his Son, purifies us from all sin.

1 JOHN 1:7 NIV

[Jesus said,] "For where two or three have gathered together in My name, I am there in their midst."

MATTHEW 18:20 NASB

///

You can develop a healthy, robust community that lives right with God and enjoy its results only if you do the hard work of getting along with each other, treating each other with dignity and honor.

JAMES 3:18 The Message

///

Love one another with mutual affection; outdo one another in showing honor.

ROMANS 12:10 NRSV

Make every effort to do what leads to peace and to mutual edification.

ROMANS 14:19 NIV

When people sin, you should forgive and comfort them, so they won't give up in despair.

2 CORINTHIANS 2:7 CEV

FELLOWSHIP CULTIVATES COMMUNITY. YOU MAY FIND YOURSELF IN MANY COMMUNITIES—YOUR CHURCH, THE NEIGHBORHOOD YOU LIVE IN, YOUR DORM, OR YOUR WORKPLACE. NO MATTER WHAT KIND OF COMMUNITY IT IS, IT REQUIRES COMMITMENT TO MAKE IT WORK. ONLY THE HOLY SPIRIT CAN CREATE REAL FELLOWSHIP BETWEEN BELIEVERS, BUT HE CULTIVATES IT WITH THE CHOICES AND COMMITMENTS WE MAKE.

CULTIVATING COMMUNITY TAKES HONESTY.

*You are joined together with peace through the Spirit,
so make every effort to continue together in this way.*
EPHESIANS 4:3 NCV

*Carry each other's burdens, and in this way
you will fulfill the law of Christ.*
GALATIANS 6:2 NIV

*Speaking the truth in love, we will grow to become
in every respect the mature body of him
who is the head, that is, Christ.*
EPHESIANS 4:15 NIV

**No more lies, no more pretense. Tell your
neighbor the truth. In Christ's body we're all
connected to each other, after all. When you lie
to others, you end up lying to yourself.**
EPHESIANS 4:25 The Message

An honest answer is a sign of true friendship.
PROVERBS 24:26 GNT

*Brothers and sisters, if someone in your group does
something wrong, you who are spiritual should go
to that person and gently help make him right again.*
GALATIANS 6:1-2 NCV

CULTIVATING COMMUNITY REQUIRES HUMILITY AND COURTESY TOWARD ONE ANOTHER.

*Clothe yourselves with humility toward one another, because,
"God opposes the proud but shows favor to the humble."*

1 PETER 5:5 NIV

*Live in harmony with each other. Don't be too proud
to enjoy the company of ordinary people.*

ROMANS 12:16 NLT

*Give more honor to others than to yourselves.
Do not be interested only in your own life,
but be interested in the lives of others.*

PHILIPPIANS 2:3–4 NCV

*We must bear the "burden" of being considerate
of the doubts and fears of others.*

ROMANS 15:2 TLB

God's people should be bighearted and courteous.

TITUS 3:2 The Message

CULTIVATING COMMUNITY TAKES CONFIDENTIALITY—
AVOID GOSSIP AT ALL COSTS. COMMUNITY ALSO
TAKES FREQUENCY—YOU HAVE TO SPEND TIME
TOGETHER OFTEN TO BUILD GREAT FRIENDSHIPS.

Gossip is spread by wicked people;
they stir up trouble and break up friendships.
PROVERBS 16:28 GNT

Warn a divisive person once, and then warn them a
second time. After that, have nothing to do with them.
TITUS 3:10 NIV

[The first Christians] worshiped together regularly at
the Temple each day, met in small groups in homes
for Communion, and shared their meals
with great joy and thankfulness.
ACTS 2:46 TLB

YOU WERE FORMED FOR GOD'S FAMILY AND FOR REGULAR, INTIMATE, DEEP FELLOWSHIP WITH OTHER BELIEVERS IN JESUS.

Be kind and compassionate to one another, forgiving each other, just as in Christ God forgave you. Follow God's example, therefore, as dearly loved children and walk in the way of love, just as Christ loved us and gave himself up for us as a fragrant offering and sacrifice to God.

EPHESIANS 4:32–5:2 NIV

///

Let the peace of Christ rule in your hearts, since as members of one body you were called to peace.

COLOSSIANS 3:15 NIV

///

If one part of the body suffers, all the other parts suffer with it. Or if one part of our body is honored, all the other parts share its honor.

1 CORINTHIANS 12:26 NCV

[Jesus said,] "Your love for one another will prove to the world that you are my disciples."

JOHN 13:35 NLT

Search for peace, and work to maintain it.
1 PETER 3:11 NLT

*Do everything possible on your part
to live in peace with everybody.*
ROMANS 12:18 GNT

*Live in harmony with each other. Let there be no
divisions in the church. Rather, be of one mind, united
in thought and purpose.*
1 CORINTHIANS 1:10 NLT

*Let us concentrate on the things which make for harmony,
and on the growth of one another's character.*
ROMANS 14:19 PHILLIPS

*You're blessed when you can show people how to
cooperate instead of compete or fight.
That's when you discover who you really are,
and your place in God's family.*
MATTHEW 5:9 The Message

God deeply desires that we experience oneness and harmony with each other. If you've ever been a part of a team, whether it be a sports team or a project team at work or school, you know that all the members must work toward the same goal or nothing gets done. Unity is the soul of fellowship.

We proclaim to you what we have seen and heard [about Jesus]
so that you also may have fellowship with us. And our fellowship is
with the Father and with his Son, Jesus Christ.

1 JOHN 1:3 NIV

[Jesus] came and preached peace to
you who were far away and peace to
those who were near. For through him we
both have access to the Father by one
Spirit. Consequently, you are no longer
foreigners and aliens, but fellow citizens
with God's people and members of God's
household, built on the foundation of the
apostles and prophets, with Christ Jesus
himself as the chief cornerstone.

EPHESIANS 2:17–20 NIV

[Jesus prayed,] "My prayer is not for [my disciples] alone.
I pray also for those who will believe in me through their message,
that all of them may be one, Father, just as you are in me
and I am in you. May they also be in us so that the world may
believe that you have sent me."

JOHN 17:20–21 NIV

FELLOWSHIP, BEING ADOPTED
AS A PART OF GOD'S FAMILY,
IS THE SECOND GREAT
PURPOSE FOR YOUR LIFE.

YOU WERE CREATED TO BECOME LIKE CHRIST!

From the very beginning God decided that those who came to him—and all along he knew who would—should become like his Son, so that his Son would be the First, with many brothers.*

ROMANS 8:29 TLB

THE THIRD REASON GOD CREATED YOU WAS
TO BECOME LIKE HIS SON, JESUS. THIS HAS BEEN
GOD'S PLAN FROM THE BEGINNING OF TIME.
IN GENESIS 1:26, GOD SAYS, "LET US MAKE MANKIND
IN OUR IMAGE" (NIV). AT THE DAWN OF THE WORLD,
GOD PLANNED FOR YOU TO HAVE THE CHARACTER
OF CHRIST—TO BE GODLY.

*You were . . . created to be like God, with a life that
truly has God's approval and is holy.*

EPHESIANS 4:24 GW

*[God] has saved us and called us to a holy life—not
because of anything we have done but because of his
own purpose and grace. This grace was given us in
Christ Jesus before the beginning of time.*

2 TIMOTHY 1:9 NIV

*We look at this Son and see God's
original purpose in everything created.*

COLOSSIANS 1:15 The Message

We were made with the very breath of God.

The LORD God formed a man from the dust of the ground and breathed into his nostrils the breath of life, and the man became a living being.

GENESIS 2:7 NIV

Because you were created to be like Christ, God is more interested in what you are than in what you do. You're not taking your diplomas or earnings or awards into heaven, but you are taking your character.

Do not store up for yourselves treasures on earth, where moths and vermin destroy, and where thieves break in and steal. But store up for yourselves treasures in heaven, where moths and vermin do not destroy, and where thieves do not break in and steal. For where your treasure is, there your heart will be also.

MATTHEW 6:19–21 NIV

Take on an entirely new way of life— a God-fashioned life, a life renewed from the inside and working itself into your conduct as God accurately reproduces his character in you.

EPHESIANS 4:24 The Message

In keeping with [God's] promise we are looking forward to a new heaven and a new earth, where righteousness dwells. So then, dear friends, since you are looking forward to this, make every effort to be found spotless, blameless and at peace with him.

2 PETER 3:13–14 NIV

Make every effort to add to your faith goodness; and to goodness, knowledge; and to knowledge, self-control; and to self-control, perseverance; and to perseverance, godliness; and to godliness, mutual affection; and to mutual affection, love.

2 PETER 1:5–7 NIV

And the Lord—who is the Spirit—makes us more and more like him as we are changed into his glorious image.

2 CORINTHIANS 3:18 NLT

God is working in you, giving you the desire and the power to do what pleases him.

PHILIPPIANS 2:13 NLT

If God wants to make us like Jesus, the question becomes, "What is Jesus like?" If you want a perfect picture of Jesus, you can find it in Galatians 5:22–23: *"The Holy Spirit produces this kind of fruit in our lives: love, joy, peace, patience, kindness, goodness, faithfulness, gentleness and self-control"* (NLT).

Those nine qualities are a picture of Jesus, and so God wants to build those nine qualities into your life.

So how does God do it? How do we become like Jesus? We don't just walk down the street one day and . . . zap! We're full of love. And we don't go to a conference and . . . bang! Suddenly we're filled with patience.

No. God does not zap. There's no such thing as instant spiritual maturity. So how does God make me like Christ?

Love

It's easy to love lovely people. God teaches you real love by putting you around some unlovely people.

Joy

Joy is different than happiness. Happiness depends on circumstances. I go to Disneyland, I'm happy. I go home and realize how much I spent, I'm not happy. Joy is internal. Happiness is external. God will teach you real joy in the middle of grief.

GOD MAKES YOU LIKE JESUS BY PUTTING YOU IN THE SITUATIONS THAT ARE COMPLETELY CONTRARY TO THE QUALITIES HE WANTS YOU TO DEVELOP.

Rejoice . . . as you participate in the sufferings of Christ,
so that you may be overjoyed when his glory is revealed.
If you are insulted because of the name of Christ, you are
blessed, for the Spirit of glory and of God rests on you.

1 PETER 4:13–14 NIV

Our light and momentary troubles are achieving for
us an eternal glory that far outweighs them all.

2 CORINTHIANS 4:17 NIV

[Jesus said,] "In this world you will have trouble.
But take heart! I have overcome the world."

JOHN 16:33 NIV

Peace

Where do you learn peace? Out fishing on a beautiful stream?
Anybody can be peaceful in that kind of environment. So instead,
God will put you in traffic jams. He'll give you a day when you have
a pop quiz and a rush project and your friend wants to borrow
money that you don't have and your computer crashes and your
car breaks down and everything's going wrong. And it is there, in
the middle of the storm, that you learn peace.

We know that God causes everything to work together for
the good of those who love God and are called according to
his purpose for them. For God knew his people in advance,
and he chose them to become like his Son.

ROMANS 8:28–29 NLT

When you pass through the waters,
I will be with you;
and when you pass through the rivers,
they will not sweep over you.
When you walk through the fire,
you will not be burned;
the flames will not set you ablaze.

ISAIAH 43:2 NIV

Patience

God's plan for teaching us patience is pretty obvious. He'll put you in doctor's offices and long lines at the DMV.

There was a time in my life when I said, "Oh God! I need patience," and instead of my struggles getting better, they got worse. Finally, after about six months, I realized I was a lot more patient than when I started. God was giving me the patience I asked for through those situations.

We also glory in our sufferings, because we know
that suffering produces perseverance; perseverance,
character; and character, hope.

ROMANS 5:3–4 NIV

Don't try to get out of anything prematurely. Let it do its work so you become mature and well-developed.

JAMES 1:4 The Message

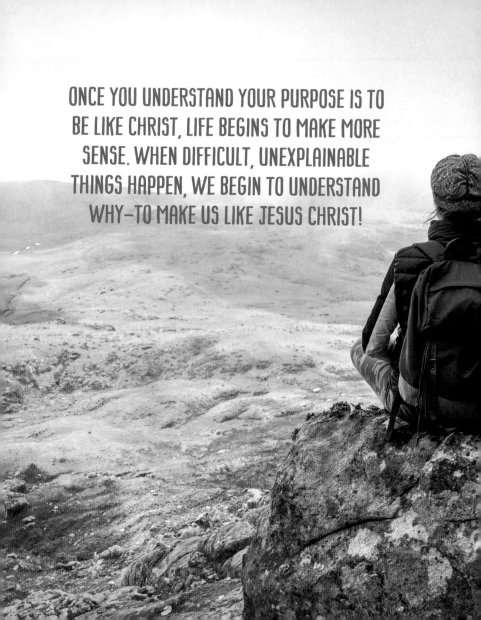

ONCE YOU UNDERSTAND YOUR PURPOSE IS TO BE LIKE CHRIST, LIFE BEGINS TO MAKE MORE SENSE. WHEN DIFFICULT, UNEXPLAINABLE THINGS HAPPEN, WE BEGIN TO UNDERSTAND WHY—TO MAKE US LIKE JESUS CHRIST!

As God works in you to make you like his Son, he is going to take you through the struggles Jesus experienced.

Were there times when Jesus was lonely?

Yes.

Were there times when Jesus was tired?

Yes.

Were there times when he was misunderstood and criticized unjustly?

Yes.

Did God take care of and strengthen Jesus through it all?

Yes. And he'll do the same for you.

*In your lives you must think
and act like Christ Jesus.*

PHILIPPIANS 2:5 NCV

*Make every effort to enter through the narrow
door [to follow Christ], because many, I tell you,
will try to enter and will not be able to.*

LUKE 13:24 NIV

No matter how difficult the situation, you can learn from it if you will respond to it with the question, "What does Jesus want me to learn?"

While effort has nothing to do with your salvation, it has much to do with your spiritual growth. We must cooperate with the Holy Spirit's work in our lives. At least eight times in the New Testament we are told to "make every effort" in our growth toward becoming like Jesus.

Make every effort to give yourself to God as the kind of person he will approve. Be a worker who is not ashamed and who uses the true teaching in the right way.

2 TIMOTHY 2:15 NCV

Make every effort to live in peace with everyone and to be holy; without holiness no one will see the Lord.

HEBREWS 12:14 NIV

We have three responsibilities in becoming like Christ.

First, we must choose to let go of old ways of acting.

> *Everything—and I do mean everything—connected with that old way of life has to go. It's rotten through and through. Get rid of it!*
>
> EPHESIANS 4:22 The Message

Second, we must change the way we think.

> *Let the Spirit change your way of thinking.*
>
> EPHESIANS 4:23 CEV

Third, we must "put on" the character of Christ by developing new, godly habits.

> *Put on the new self, created to be like God in true righteousness and holiness.*
>
> EPHESIANS 4:24 NIV

*As you come to [Christ,] the living Stone—rejected by
humans but chosen by God and precious to him—you
also, like living stones, are being built into a spiritual
house to be a holy priesthood, offering spiritual
sacrifices acceptable to God through Jesus Christ.
For in Scripture it says:
"See, I lay a stone in Zion, a chosen and
precious cornerstone, and the one who trusts
in him will never be put to shame."*

1 PETER 2:4–6 NIV

God's third purpose for your life, the process that God uses to
make you like Jesus, is called Discipleship. God wants you to
become a mature member of his family, just as Christ is.

*I want to know Christ—yes, to know the power of
his resurrection and participation in his sufferings,
becoming like him in his death, and so, somehow,
attaining to the resurrection from the dead.*

PHILIPPIANS 3:10–11 NIV

*We are transfigured much like the Messiah, our lives
gradually becoming brighter and more beautiful as
God enters our lives and we become like him.*

2 CORINTHIANS 3:18 The Message

Discipleship—the process of becoming like Christ—always begins with a decision.

> *"Follow me and be my disciple," Jesus said to him.*
> *So Matthew got up and followed him.*
> MATTHEW 9:9 NLT

Once you decide to get serious about becoming like Christ, you must begin to act in new ways. You can be certain that the Holy Spirit will help you with these changes.

> *Continue to work out your salvation with fear and*
> *trembling, for it is God who works in you to will*
> *and to act in order to fulfill to his good purpose.*
> PHILIPPIANS 2:12–13 NIV

The "work out" is your responsibility, and the "work in" is God's role.

YOUR FIRST STEP IN SPIRITUAL GROWTH IS TO START CHANGING THE WAY YOU THINK. THE WAY YOU THINK DETERMINES THE WAY YOU FEEL, AND THE WAY YOU FEEL INFLUENCES THE WAY YOU ACT.

> *Let God transform you into a new person*
> *by changing the way you think.*
> ROMANS 12:2 NLT

Let the Spirit renew your thoughts and attitudes.

EPHESIANS 4:23 NLT

///

Be careful how you think;
your life is shaped by your thoughts.

PROVERBS 4:23 GNT

///

*Stop thinking like children. In regard to evil be infants,
but in your thinking be adults.*

1 CORINTHIANS 14:20 NIV

*Those who live following their sinful selves think only about things
that their sinful selves want. But those who live following the Spirit
are thinking about the things the Spirit wants them to do.*

ROMANS 8:5 NCV

*When I was a child, I talked like a child, I thought like
a child, I reasoned like a child. When I became a man,
I put the ways of childhood behind me.*

1 CORINTHIANS 13:11 NIV

*God has given us his Spirit. That's why we don't think
the same way that the people of this world think.*

1 CORINTHIANS 2:12 CEV

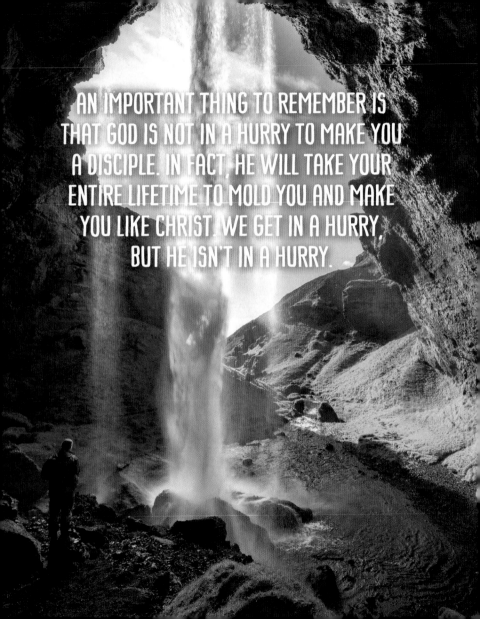

AN IMPORTANT THING TO REMEMBER IS THAT GOD IS NOT IN A HURRY TO MAKE YOU A DISCIPLE. IN FACT, HE WILL TAKE YOUR ENTIRE LIFETIME TO MOLD YOU AND MAKE YOU LIKE CHRIST. WE GET IN A HURRY, BUT HE ISN'T IN A HURRY.

Often we get discouraged and think, "I'm not growing. I'm not going fast enough." But God has promised to never give up on us. The Bible has promised:

Everything on earth has its own time and its own season.
ECCLESIASTES 3:1 CEV

You have begun to live the new life, in which you are being made new and are becoming like the One who made you.
COLOSSIANS 3:10 NCV

God who began a good work in us will bring it to the day of completion.
PHILIPPIANS 1:6 NJB

Spiritual maturity is neither instant nor automatic; it is a gradual, progressive development that will take the rest of your life. Becoming like Christ is a long, slow process of growth.

He has not yet shown us what we will be like when Christ appears. But we do know that we will be like him, for we will see him as he really is.
1 JOHN 3:2 NLT

Don't become so well-adjusted to your culture that you fit into it without even thinking. Instead, fix your attention on God. You'll be changed from the inside out. . . . Unlike the culture around you, always dragging you down to its level of immaturity, God brings the best out of you, develops well-formed maturity in you.
ROMANS 12:2 The Message

Although God could instantly transform us, he has chosen to develop us slowly. Why does it take so long to change and grow up?

We are slow learners.

You were taught, with regard to your former way of life, to put off your old self, which is being corrupted by its deceitful desires; to be made new in the attitude of your minds.

EPHESIANS 4:22–23 NIV

We have a lot to unlearn.

Now you must also rid yourselves of all such things as these: anger, rage, malice, slander, and filthy language from your lips. Do not lie to each other, since you have taken off your old self with its practices and have put on the new self, which is being renewed in knowledge in the image of its Creator.

COLOSSIANS 3:8–10 NIV

Habits take time to develop.

Practice [spiritual disciplines]. Devote your life to them so that everyone can see your progress.

1 TIMOTHY 4:15 GW

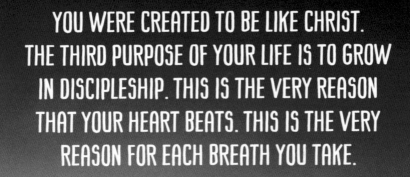

YOU WERE CREATED TO BE LIKE CHRIST.
THE THIRD PURPOSE OF YOUR LIFE IS TO GROW
IN DISCIPLESHIP. THIS IS THE VERY REASON
THAT YOUR HEART BEATS. THIS IS THE VERY
REASON FOR EACH BREATH YOU TAKE.

YOU WERE SHAPED
FOR SERVING GOD!

*God has made us what we are. In Christ Jesus, God
made us to do good works, which God planned in
advance for us to live our lives doing.*

EPHESIANS 2:10 NCV

Whenever God gives us an assignment, he always equips us with what we need to accomplish it. This custom combination of capabilities is called your S.H.A.P.E.

S.H.A.P.E. stands for:

S—**Spiritual Gifts**: Special gifts given by the Holy Spirit so you can help build up the church.

H—**Heart**: Special passions, things that you feel strongly about, to drive you to service.

A—**Abilities**: Natural talents built into you from birth.

P—**Personality**: Your uniqueness, what makes you different from everyone else.

E—**Experiences**: Situations and circumstances you face that help you empathize with others.

God has wired you with these five things to make you *you*.

Your hands shaped me and made me.

JOB 10:8 NIV

*You made all the delicate, inner parts of my body
and knit me together in my mother's womb.
Thank you for making me so wonderfully complex!
Your workmanship is marvelous.*

PSALM 139:13–14 NLT

Spiritual Gifts

These are God-empowered abilities for serving him that are given only to believers.

We have different gifts, according to the grace given to each of us. If your gift is prophesying, then prophesy in accordance with your faith; if it is serving, then serve; if it is teaching, then teach; if it is to encourage, then give encouragement; if it is giving, then give generously; if it is to lead, do it diligently; if it is to show mercy, do it cheerfully.

ROMANS 12:6–8 NIV

So Christ himself gave the apostles, the prophets, the evangelists, the pastors and teachers, to equip [God's] people for works of service, so that the body of Christ may be built up.

EPHESIANS 4:11–12 NIV

A spiritual gift is given to each of us so we can help each other.

1 CORINTHIANS 12:7 NLT

There are different kinds of service, but we serve the same Lord.

1 CORINTHIANS 12:5 NLT

Heart

Your heart represents the source of all your motivations—what you love to do and what you care about most. Another word for heart is passion. Don't ignore your interests. Consider how they might be used for God's glory. There is a reason that you love to do these things.

Serve the LORD with all your heart.
1 SAMUEL 12:20 NIV

Above all else, guard your heart,
for everything you do flows from it.
PROVERBS 4:23 NIV

Abilities

Your abilities are the natural talents you were born with.

In his grace, God has given us different gifts
for doing certain things well.
ROMANS 12:6 NLT

There are different abilities to perform service, but the same God
gives ability to all for their particular service.
1 CORINTHIANS 12:6 GNT

God has given each of you some special abilities; be
sure to use them to help each other, passing on to
others God's many kinds of blessings.
1 PETER 4:10 TLB

Personality

God created each of us with a unique combination of personality traits. There is no "right" or "wrong" temperament for ministry. We need all kinds of personalities to balance the church.

God works through different men in different ways, but it is the same God who achieves his purposes through them all.

1 CORINTHIANS 12:6 PHILLIPS

Experiences

Experiences are one of the most important things that God uses to shape you for service. There are five kinds of experiences God uses:

- **Family experiences**—interactions with parents, children, spouses, and anyone you call family.

- **Vocational experiences**—everything you learn on the job, from skills to getting along with others.

- **Educational experiences**—times of learning throughout your life, from elementary school to continuing discovery as an adult.

- **Spiritual experiences**—those special moments of incredible closeness with God, when you discover something new about who he is and who you are in him.

But most important of all:

- **Painful experiences**—disappointments, hurts, and sorrows that cause you to lean heavily on God, and that develop empathy in your heart for the hurts of others.

Painful experiences are hard to understand. We ask God, "Why me?" But . . .

- Who can better help someone with cancer than someone who has battled cancer themselves?

- Who can better help somebody going through the pain of their parents' divorce than somebody else who has gone through the same thing?

- Who can better help a student with a learning disability than somebody who has also struggled with learning difficulties?

Often the very thing that you struggle most with in your life, the very thing you like the least, the very thing you're most embarrassed and ashamed of, is the very thing God wants to use to help you minister to others. God uses not just our strengths. He also uses our weaknesses.

> *[Jesus said], "My grace is sufficient for you, for my power is made perfect in weakness." Therefore I will boast all the more gladly about my weaknesses, so that Christ's power may rest on me.*
>
> 2 CORINTHIANS 12:9 NIV

Why does God use our weaknesses? Because when he does, he gets all the glory. If somebody does something great using their own obvious strengths, people see it and say, "Well, he's just good at that. Of course it will be a success." But if somebody does something wonderful in an area that is obviously not their strength, people say, "Wow! Maybe there is hope for me! If God can do that for them, he can surely do that for me!"

> For Christ's sake, I delight in weaknesses, in insults, in hardships, in persecutions, in difficulties. For when I am weak, then I am strong.
>
> 2 CORINTHIANS 12:10 NIV

God is giving you a special S.H.A.P.E. Using your special abilities, gifts, and life experiences for the benefit of others is called Ministry—the fourth purpose of your life.

God has given each of you some special abilities. Be sure to use them to help each other, passing on to others God's many kinds of blessings.

1 PETER 4:10 TLB

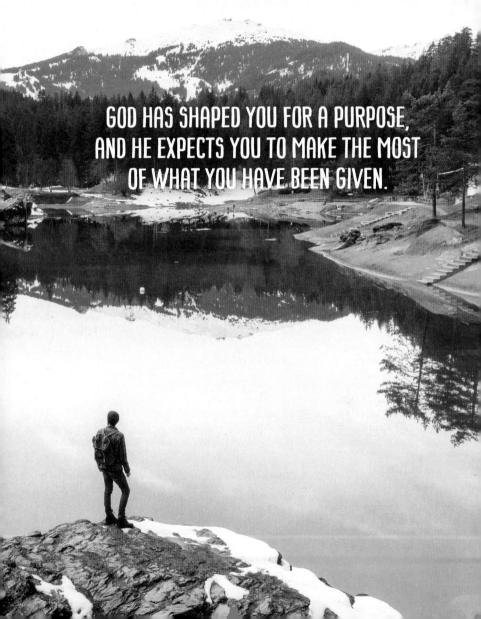

GOD HAS SHAPED YOU FOR A PURPOSE, AND HE EXPECTS YOU TO MAKE THE MOST OF WHAT YOU HAVE BEEN GIVEN.

No matter who you are, if you allow God to shape your life, you can be used by him for great things. There is one key qualification, though:

Those who make themselves clean from all . . .
evil things, will be used for special purposes, because
they are dedicated and useful to their Master,
ready to be used for every good deed.

2 TIMOTHY 2:21 GNT

God can use small vessels. God can use plain vessels. God can even use broken vessels. But he will not use a dirty vessel.

The good news is you can be clean simply by asking.

*If we confess our sins, [God] is faithful
and just and will forgive us our sins and
purify us from all unrighteousness.*

1 JOHN 1:9 NIV

To discover your shape, begin by assessing your gifts and abilities.

*Don't act thoughtlessly, but try to find out and do
whatever the Lord wants you to.*

EPHESIANS 5:17 TLB

Try to have a sane estimate of your capabilities.

ROMANS 12:3 PHILLIPS

Consider your heart and your personality.

*Make a careful exploration of who you are
and the work you have been given,
and then sink yourself into that.*
GALATIANS 6:4 The Message

Examine your experiences and extract the lessons you have learned.

*Remember today what you have learned about the
LORD through your experiences with him.*
DEUTERONOMY 11:2 GNT

Since God knows what's best for you, you should gratefully accept the way he fashioned you.

> *What right have you, a human being, to cross-examine God? The pot has no right to say to the potter: "Why did you make me this shape?" Surely a potter can do what he likes with the clay!*
>
> ROMANS 9:20–21 NJB

> *Christ has given each of us special abilities—whatever he wants us to have out of his rich storehouse of gifts.*
>
> EPHESIANS 4:7 TLB

Part of accepting your shape is recognizing your limitations. God assigns each of us a field or sphere of service.

> *Stay within the limits of the work which God has set for us.*
>
> 2 CORINTHIANS 10:13 GNT

> *Let us run with patience the particular race that God has set before us.*
>
> HEBREWS 12:1 TLB

> *Pay careful attention to your own work, for then you will get the satisfaction of a job well done, and you won't need to compare yourself to anyone else.*
>
> GALATIANS 6:4 NLT

Keep developing your shape. We are to cultivate our gifts and abilities, keep our hearts aflame, grow our character and personality, and broaden our experiences so we will be increasingly more effective in our service.

Do you like kids? Volunteer at an after-school club or to teach Sunday school. Can you sing? Join the choir or sing a solo in church. Do your interests lie in the area of business and finance? Find out if the finance committee at church has an opening. God has given you some great gifts to use for him.

*Keep on growing in knowledge
and understanding.*
PHILIPPIANS 1:9 NLT

*Concentrate on doing your best for God,
work you won't be ashamed of.*

2 TIMOTHY 2:15 The Message

Kindle afresh the gift of God which is in you.
2 TIMOTHY 1:6 NASB

*Be sure to use the abilities God has given you. . . .
Put these abilities to work.*
1 TIMOTHY 4:14–15 TLB

Like athletes preparing for the Olympics, we keep training for that big day.

They do it for a gold medal that tarnishes and fades. You're after one that's gold eternally.

1 CORINTHIANS 9:25 The Message

WE SERVE GOD BY SERVING OTHERS.
HOW CAN YOU HAVE THE HEART
OF A SERVANT?

Real servants make themselves available to serve.

No soldier in active service entangles himself in the affairs of everyday life, so that he may please the one who enlisted him.

2 TIMOTHY 2:4 NASB

Being a servant means giving up the right to control your schedule and allowing God to interrupt it whenever he needs to.

Real servants pay attention to needs.

//

Whenever we have the opportunity, we have to do what is good for everyone, especially for the family of believers.

GALATIANS 6:10 GW

//

Never tell your neighbors to wait until tomorrow if you can help them now.

PROVERBS 3:28 GNT

Real servants do every task with equal dedication.

[Jesus said,] "You call me 'Teacher' and 'Lord' and rightly so, for that is what I am. Now that I, your Lord and Teacher, have washed your feet, you also should wash one another's feet. I have set you an example that you should do as I have done for you. Very truly I tell you, no servant is greater than his master, nor is a messenger greater than the one who sent him. Now that you know these things, you will be blessed if you do them."

JOHN 13:13–17 NIV

Whoever can be trusted with very little can also be trusted with much.

LUKE 16:10 NIV

Real servants maintain a low profile.

When you do good deeds, don't try to show off. If you do, you won't get a reward from your Father in heaven.

MATTHEW 6:1 CEV

When Christ . . . shows up again on this earth, you'll show up, too—the real you, the glorious you. Meanwhile, be content with obscurity.

COLOSSIANS 3:4 The Message

God's Power in Your Weakness

We are weak . . . yet by God's power
we will live with him in our dealing with you.

2 CORINTHIANS 13:4 NIV

I am with you; that is all you need.
My power shows up best in weak people.

2 CORINTHIANS 12:9 TLB

My thoughts and my ways are higher than yours.

ISAIAH 55:9 CEV

God purposely chose . . . what the world considers
weak in order to shame the powerful.

1 CORINTHIANS 1:27 GNT

We are like clay jars in which this treasure
[of the gospel] is stored. The real power comes
from God and not from us.

2 CORINTHIANS 4:7 CEV

God loves to use weak people. We usually deny, defend, excuse, hide, or resent our weaknesses. This prevents God from using them the way he desires. God has a different perspective on your weaknesses.

The fourth purpose for your life is ministry—serving others through serving God.

You were made to minister, so when you start to get run down you can pray:

"God, light that fire again in my heart. I was planned for your pleasure, so help me to worship you. I was formed for your family, so let me fellowship. I was created to be like Christ, so keep me growing. I was shaped to serve you, so help me to be faithful in my ministry."

///

The one who calls you is faithful,
and he will do it.

1 THESSALONIANS 5:24 NIV

///

YOU WERE MADE FOR A MISSION!

*[Jesus prayed,] "In the same way that [God] gave me
a mission in the world, I give [my followers]
a mission in the world."*
JOHN 17:18 The Message

God has given us a mission in life.

*Through Christ, God has made peace between us
and Himself and He gave us the work of telling
everyone the peace we can have with Him.
So we have been sent to speak for Christ.*

2 CORINTHIANS 5:19–20 NJB

If you want God's blessing and power on your life, you must care about what God cares about most, and the biggest concern of God's heart is bringing his lost children back home to him.

*The fruit of the righteous is a tree of life,
and the one who is wise saves lives.*

PROVERBS 11:30 NIV

*God . . . through Christ changed us from
enemies into his friends and gave us
the task of making others his friends also.*

2 CORINTHIANS 5:18 GNT

The Importance of Your Mission

Fulfilling your life mission on earth is an essential part of living for God's glory. The Bible gives several reasons why your mission is so important.

1. Your mission is a continuation of Jesus' mission on earth. As his followers, we are to continue what Jesus started.

> *[Jesus said,] "Go to the people of all nations and make them my disciples. Baptize them in the name of the Father, the Son, and the Holy Spirit, and teach them to do everything I have told you."*
>
> MATTHEW 28:19–20 CEV

> *You must warn [unbelievers] so they may live. If you don't speak out to warn the wicked to stop their evil ways, they will die in their sin.*
>
> EZEKIEL 3:18 NCV

You are the only Christian some people will ever know, and your mission is to share Jesus with them.

2. Your mission is a wonderful privilege. Although it is a big responsibility, it is also an incredible honor to be used by God.

God has given us the privilege of urging everyone to come into his favor and be reconciled to him.
2 CORINTHIANS 5:18 TLB

We are workers together with God.
2 CORINTHIANS 6:1 NCV

We're Christ's representatives. God uses us to persuade men and women to drop their differences and enter into God's work of making things right between them. We are speaking for Christ himself now: Become friends with God.
2 CORINTHIANS 5:20 The Message

3. Telling others how they can have eternal life is the greatest thing you can do for them. Everybody needs Jesus.

Jesus is the only One who can save people.
ACTS 4:12 NCV

4. Your mission has eternal significance. It will impact the eternal destiny of other people, so it's more important than any job, achievement, or goal you will reach during your life on earth.

We must quickly carry out the tasks assigned us by the one who sent us. The night is coming, and then no one can work.

JOHN 9:4 NLT

5. Your mission gives your life meaning.

My life is worth nothing to me unless I use it for finishing the work assigned me by the Lord Jesus—the work of telling others the Good News about the wonderful grace of God.

ACTS 20:24 NLT

6. God's timetable for history's conclusion is connected to the completion of our commission. Jesus will not return until everyone God wants to hear the Good News has heard it.

About that day or hour [of my return] no one knows, not even the angels in heaven, nor the Son, but only the Father."

MATTHEW 24:36 NIV

Jesus said . . . "As the Father has sent me, I am sending you."

JOHN 20:21 NIV

Jesus said, "It is not for you to know the times or dates the Father has set by his own authority. But you will receive power when the Holy Spirit comes on you; and you will be my witnesses in Jerusalem, and in all Judea and Samaria, and to the ends of the earth."

ACTS 1:7–8 NIV

The Good News about God's kingdom will be preached in all the world, to every nation. Then the end will come.

MATTHEW 24:14 NCV

Our mission on earth is to be ambassadors for God! God loves us so much that he has sent us to represent him to people who don't know him. That is your mission to the world.

We have been sent to speak for Christ.

2 CORINTHIANS 5:20 NCV

///

The most important thing is that I complete my mission, the work that the Lord Jesus gave me—to tell people the Good News about God's grace.

ACTS 20:24 NCV

///

God so loved the world that he gave his one and only Son, that whoever believes in him shall not perish but have eternal life.

JOHN 3:16 NIV

Fulfilling your mission in the world is called evangelism—the fifth purpose of your life.

Once you become part of God's family, it's your mission to tell others so they can join you, for God doesn't want anyone to be outside of his family.

Through Christ, all the kindness of God has been poured out upon us undeserving sinners; and now he is sending us out around the world to tell all people everywhere the great things God has done for them, so they, too, will believe and obey him.

ROMANS 1:5 TLB

The Lord is not slow in keeping his promise, as some understand slowness. Instead he is patient with you, not wanting anyone to perish, but everyone to come to repentance.

2 PETER 3:9 NIV

ONE MORE

My dad was a man on a mission. He was a pastor for 50 years. He was also a carpenter. He volunteered his time to build over 150 church buildings around the world, on every continent. He would take disaster teams to South America, the North Pole, Iraq, Jerusalem—all around the world. Even in his seventies he was up on rooftops, building churches in Siberia.

My dad died of cancer. The last week of his life, he was in a dream-like state, and he talked constantly, and in that last week, I listened to my dad dream aloud. You can learn a lot about a person by listening to their dreams.

He didn't talk about the movies he'd seen or the books he'd read. He didn't talk about his escapades in the South Pacific during World War II. He didn't talk about fishing, which he dearly loved. He talked about the deepest passion of his heart— building churches.

As he dreamed he would say aloud: "You take those two-by-fours over to that corner and make sure that joist is correct. Don't get electrocuted! Make sure they get back for lunch."

One evening, just before he died, when he was at his weakest state, my dad became very agitated, and he tried to get out of bed. My wife tried to comfort him: "No, Jimmy, you've got to lay down. You're very weak. You need to lay down."

Still, he continued to struggle to get out of bed. She said, "Jimmy, what do you want?"

He said, "Got to save one more for Jesus. Got to save one more for Jesus."

Over and over, for the next hour, he repeated this phrase. "Got to save one more for Jesus! Save one more for Jesus! Save one more for Jesus!"

I put my head down on the side of his bed and tears were coming down my face. He reached up and put his hands on my head, and he said, "Save one more for Jesus! Save one more for Jesus."

I intend for that phrase to be the theme of the rest of my life. I invite you to make it the theme for your life, too. As you consider what you will do for the rest of your life, I can assure you there is nothing more important than bringing people to Jesus.

Our mission on earth is to be ambassadors for God! God loves us so much that he has sent us to represent him to people who don't know him. That is your mission to the world.

This is our mission—bringing people to Christ so they can be built up to maturity, be trained for a ministry, be equipped for their life mission, and live a life for the glory of God.

I challenge you—reach one more for Jesus.

Sharing Your Life Message

Those who believe in the Son of God
have the testimony of God in them.

1 JOHN 5:10 GW

Your lives are echoing the Master's Word. . . . The
news of your faith in God is out. We don't even have
to say anything anymore—you're the message!

1 THESSALONIANS 1:8 The Message

In Christ we speak the truth before God, as messengers of God.

2 CORINTHIANS 2:17 NCV

You are the ones chosen by God, chosen for the high
calling of priestly work, chosen to be a holy people,
God's instruments to do his work and speak out
for him, to tell others of the night-and-day difference
he made for you—from nothing to something,
from rejected to accepted.

1 PETER 2:9–10 The Message

Be ready at all times to answer anyone who asks
you to explain the hope you have in you,
but do it with gentleness and respect.

1 PETER 3:15–16 GNT

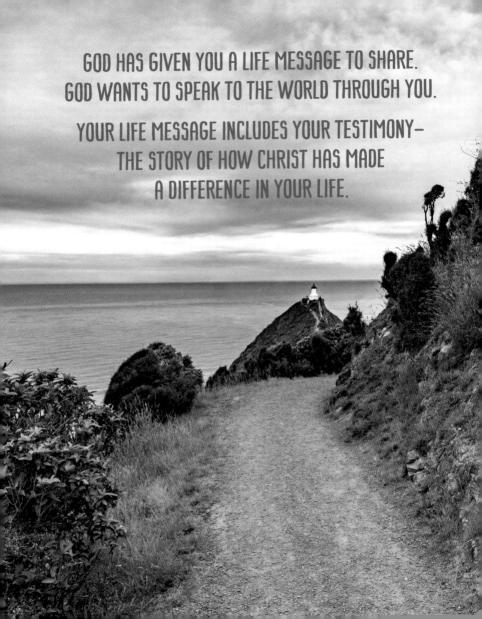

GOD HAS GIVEN YOU A LIFE MESSAGE TO SHARE.
GOD WANTS TO SPEAK TO THE WORLD THROUGH YOU.

YOUR LIFE MESSAGE INCLUDES YOUR TESTIMONY—
THE STORY OF HOW CHRIST HAS MADE
A DIFFERENCE IN YOUR LIFE.

BE READY

The best way to "be ready" is to write out your testimony and then memorize the main points. Divide it into four parts:

1. What my life was like before I met Jesus

2. How I realized I needed Jesus

3. How I committed my life to Jesus

4. The difference Jesus has made in my life

Your Life Message includes your life lessons—the truths that God has taught you from experiences with him.

> *God, teach me lessons for living*
> *so I can stay the course.*
> PSALM 119:33 The Message

> *A warning given by an experienced person to*
> *someone willing to listen is more valuable than . . .*
> *jewelry made of the finest gold.*
> PROVERBS 25:12 GNT

Your Life Message includes sharing your godly passions—as you grow closer to God, he will give you a passion for something he cares about deeply so you can be a spokesman for him in the world.

Mature people develop the habit of extracting lessons from everyday experiences. Make a list of your life lessons. Here a few questions to get you started:

What has God taught me . . .

- From failure?
- From a lack of money?
- From pain or sorrow or depression?
- Through waiting?
- From disappointment?
- From my family, my church, my relationships, my small group, and my critics?

A man's heart determines his speech.
MATTHEW 12:34 TLB

My zeal for God and his work burns hot within me.
PSALM 69:9 TLB

Your message burns in my heart and bones,
and I cannot keep silent.
JEREMIAH 20:9 CEV

God gives us different passions so that everything he wants done in the world will get done.

Your Life Message includes the Good News—that when we trust God's grace to save us through what Jesus did, our sins are forgiven, we get a purpose for living, and we are promised a future home in heaven.

The Good News shows how God makes people right with himself—that it begins and ends with faith.

ROMANS 1:17 NCV

God was in Christ, reconciling the world to himself, no longer counting people's sins against them. And he gave us this wonderful message of reconciliation.

2 CORINTHIANS 5:19 NLT

Christ's love compels us, because we are convinced that one died for all.

2 CORINTHIANS 5:14 NIV

God has never made a person he didn't love. Everybody matters to him. When Jesus stretched out his arms wide on the cross, he was saying, "I love you this much!" Whenever you feel apathetic about your mission in the world, spend some time thinking about what Jesus did for you on the cross.

If you've been afraid to share the Good News with those around you, ask God to fill your heart with his love for them.

There is no fear in love; perfect love drives out all fear.
1 JOHN 4:18 GNT

[God] does not want anyone to be lost, but he wants all people to change their hearts and lives.

2 PETER 3:9 NCV

Make the most of your chances to tell others the Good News. Be wise in all your contacts with them.
COLOSSIANS 4:5 TLB

Is anyone going to be in heaven because of you? Imagine the joy of greeting people in heaven whom you helped get there!

YOU HAVE A CHOICE TO MAKE

You will either be a world-class Christian or a worldly Christian. Worldly Christians look to God primarily for personal fulfillment. They are saved, but self-centered. It's a "me-first" faith: How can God make my life more comfortable? They want to use God for their purposes instead of being used for his purposes.

In contrast, world-class Christians know they were saved to serve and made for a mission. They are eager to receive a personal assignment and excited about the privilege of being used by God. World-class Christians are the only fully alive people on the planet. Their joy, confidence, and enthusiasm are contagious because they know they're making a difference.

What type of Christian do you want to be?

HOW TO THINK LIKE A WORLD-CLASS CHRISTIAN

1. Shift from self-centered thinking to other-centered thinking.

My friends, stop thinking like children.
Think like mature people.

1 CORINTHIANS 14:20 CEV

This is the first step to becoming a world-class Christian. Children only think of themselves; grown-ups think of others.

Don't look out only for your own interests,
but take an interest in others, too.

PHILIPPIANS 2:4 NLT

The only way we can make this switch is by a moment-by-moment dependence on God. Fortunately he doesn't leave us to struggle on our own.

God has given us his Spirit. That's why we don't think
the same way that the people of this world think.

1 CORINTHIANS 2:12 CEV

I don't think about what would be good for me but
about what would be good for many people so that
they might be saved.

1 CORINTHIANS 10:33 GW

YOUR GOAL IS TO FIGURE OUT WHERE OTHERS ARE IN THEIR SPIRITUAL JOURNEY AND THEN DO WHATEVER WILL BRING THEM A STEP CLOSER TO KNOWING CHRIST.

2. Shift from local thinking to global thinking.

God is a global God. He has always cared about the entire world.

> *From one person God made all nations who live on earth, and he decided when and where every nation would be. God has done all this, so that we will look for him and reach out and find him.*
>
> ACTS 17:26–27 CEV

The first way to start thinking globally is to begin praying for specific countries. World-class Christians pray for the world. Get a globe or a map and pray for nations by name.

> *If you ask me, I will give you the nations; all the people on earth will be yours.*
>
> PSALM 2:8 NCV

What should you pray for? The Bible tells us to pray for opportunities to witness, for courage to speak up, for those who will believe, for the rapid spread of the message, and for more workers.

The best way to switch to global thinking is to just get up and go on a short-term mission project to another country! There's simply no substitute for hands-on, real life experience in another culture.

> *You will tell everyone about me in Jerusalem, in all Judea, in Samaria, and everywhere in the world.*
>
> ACTS 1:8 CEV

3. Shift from "here and now" thinking to eternal thinking.

To make the most of your time on earth, you must maintain an eternal perspective. This will keep you from majoring on minor issues and help you distinguish between what's urgent and what's ultimate.

We fix our eyes not on what is seen, but on what is unseen, since what is seen is temporary, but what is unseen is eternal.

2 CORINTHIANS 4:18 NIV

Deal as sparingly as possible with the things the world thrusts on you. This world as you see it is fading away.

1 CORINTHIANS 7:31 The Message

What's keeping you from being a world-class Christian? Whatever it is, let it go.

Let us strip off anything that slows us down or holds us back.

HEBREWS 12:1 TLB

You've probably heard the expression "You can't take it with you"— but the Bible says you can send it on ahead by investing in people who are going there!

By doing this they will be storing up real treasure for themselves in in heaven—it is the only safe investment for eternity! And they will be living a fruitful Christian life down here as well.

1 TIMOTHY 6:19 TLB

4. Shift from thinking of excuses to thinking of creative ways to fulfill your commission.

Whether it was Sarah claiming she was too old to be used by God or Jeremiah claiming he was too young, God rejected their excuses.

> *You must go wherever I send you and say whatever*
> *I tell you. And don't be afraid of the people,*
> *for I will be with you and will protect you.*
> JEREMIAH 1:7–8 NLT

Maybe you have believed that you needed a special "call" from God, and you've been waiting for some supernatural feeling or experience. But God has already stated his call repeatedly. We are all called to fulfill God's five purposes for our lives: to worship, to fellowship, to grow like Christ, to serve, and to be on a mission with God in the world. God doesn't want to use just some of his people; he wants to use all of his people.

There are over 7 billion people on earth, and Jesus wants all his lost children found.

> *Only those who throw away their lives for my sake*
> *and for the sake of the Good News will ever know*
> *what it means to really live.*
> MARK 8:35 TLB

BALANCING YOUR LIFE

Blessed are the balanced; they shall outlast everyone. Your life is a pentathlon of five purposes, which you must keep in balance. Keeping these five purposes in balance is not easy. We all tend to overemphasize the purposes we feel most passionate about and neglect the others.

If you are serious about staying on track, you will need to develop four important habits.

1. Talk through your spiritual life and its progress with a spiritual partner or small group.

As iron sharpens iron,
so people can improve each other.
PROVERBS 27:17 NCV

We learn best in community. Our minds are sharpened and our convictions are deepened through conversation. Remember we are meant to grow together, not separately.

Encourage each other and give each other strength.
1 THESSALONIANS 5:11 NCV

2. Give yourself a regular spiritual check-up.

God places a high value on the habit of self-evaluation. At least five times in Scripture we are told to test and examine our own spiritual health.

> *Test yourselves to make sure you are solid in the faith. Don't drift along taking everything for granted. Give yourselves regular checkups. . . . Test it out. If you fail the test, do something about it.*
>
> 2 CORINTHIANS 13:5 The Message

For your spiritual health you need to regularly check the five vital signs of worship, fellowship, growth in character, ministry, and mission. You can use the "Purpose Driven Health Assessment" on the next three pages to help you do your own spiritual health checkup.

A GREAT COMMITMENT TO THE GREAT COMMANDMENT AND THE GREAT COMMISSION WILL MAKE YOU A GREAT CHRISTIAN.

PURPOSE DRIVEN HEALTH ASSESSMENT

(Rate each statement with a number, 1–5. 1 means "I'm just beginning on this," 3 means "I'm getting going," and 5 means "I am well developed in this area.")

WORSHIP: YOU WERE PLANNED FOR GOD'S PLEASURE.

_ I am experiencing more of the presence and power of God in my everyday life.

_ I am faithfully attending my small group and weekend services to worship God.

_ I am seeking to please God by surrendering to him every area of my life (health, decisions, finances, relationships, future, etc.).

_ I am accepting the things I cannot change and becoming more grateful for the life God has given me.

FELLOWSHIP: YOU WERE FORMED FOR GOD'S FAMILY.

_ I am deepening my understanding of and friendship with God in community with others.

_ I am growing in my ability both to share and to show my love to others.

_ I am willing to share my real needs for prayer and support from others.

_ I am resolving conflict constructively and am willing to forgive others.

DISCIPLESHIP: YOU WERE CREATED TO BECOME LIKE CHRIST.

_ I have a growing relationship with God through regular time reading the Bible and praying (spiritual habits).

_ I am experiencing more of the characteristics of Jesus Christ (love, joy, peace, patience, kindness, self-control, etc.) in my life.

_ I am avoiding addictive behaviors (too much food, screen time, busyness, and the like) to meet my needs.

_ I am spending time with a Christian friend (spiritual partner) who celebrates and challenges my spiritual growth.

MINISTRY: YOU WERE SHAPED FOR SERVING GOD.

_ I have discovered and am further developing my unique God-given shape for ministry.

_ I am regularly asking God to show me opportunities to serve him and others.

_ I am serving in a regular (once a month or more) ministry in the church or community.

_ I am a team player in my small group by sharing some group role or responsibility.

EVANGELISM: YOU WERE MADE FOR A MISSION.

_ I am cultivating relationships with non-Christians and asking God to give me opportunities to share his love.

_ I am investing my time in another person or group who needs to know Christ personally.

_ I am regularly inviting unchurched or unconnected friends to my church or small group.

_ I am praying and learning about where God can use me and our group cross-culturally for missions.

Total your answers in each individual section and use this guide to evaluate how you're doing and where you need to improve:

Just Beginning	0–5
Fair	5–10
Getting Going	10–15
Very Good	15–20
Well Developed	20–25

THE MORE YOU KNOW, THE MORE GOD EXPECTS YOU TO USE THAT KNOWLEDGE TO HELP OTHERS.

AVOIDING THE ENVY TRAP

I observed all the work and ambition
motivated by envy. What a waste!
ECCLESIASTES 4:4 The Message

Having ambitious dreams, a desire to be better, and faith goals
are all good things, if they come from God, benefit others, and
are pursued in faith for his glory. You should want to make the
most of your life, create beauty, and help others. But envy poisons
everything it touches and prevents God's blessing on your efforts.

Solomon wrote,

It is better to be satisfied with what you have
than to be always wanting something else.
ECCLESIASTES 6:9 GNT

As humans, we are naturally interested in how others look, act, talk,
and live. We notice what they wear, what they do, and what they
have. We grow up comparing everything: appearance, grades,
athletic ability, and other talents. But God says these comparisons
are foolish. He doesn't judge you for talents you don't have or for
opportunities you didn't get. He evaluates your faithfulness by
how you lived and what you did with what you were given.

Isn't everything you have and everything you are sheer gifts from
God? So what's the point of all this comparing and competing?
You already have all you need.
1 CORINTHIANS 4:7–8 The Message

Why is envy harmful?

Envy blinds you to the amazing value of your own unique shape.
Envy distracts you from God's custom-made plan for you.
Envy is the enemy of contentment.
Envy causes "disorder" in your life.

*Anyone who lets himself be distracted from the work
I plan for him is not fit for the Kingdom of God.*

LUKE 9:62 TLB

*Where you have envy and selfish ambition,
there you find disorder and every evil practice.*

JAMES 3:16 NIV

Tips for Staying Away from Envy

1. Train yourself to refocus on something else whenever you are tempted to compare.
2. Learn to enjoy the successes and joys of others.
3. Choose to be happy with what you have and who you are.
4. Be thankful for what you've got.
5. Trust that God is fair, and he knows what's best for you.

God never creates clones, never copies what he's already made, and never duplicates a life plan. God only creates original masterpieces, and he distinctively shaped you for a life unlike any other.

We are God's masterpiece.

EPHESIANS 2:10 NLT

Only you can live the life God designed *you* to live.

THE PEOPLE-PLEASER TRAP

I'm not trying to win the approval of people,
but of God. If pleasing people were my goal,
I would not be Christ's servant.

GALATIANS 1:10 NLT

There is nothing wrong with our desire to be accepted, appreciated, and approved by other people. In fact, without the affirmation of others we never wholly blossom into our full potential. The dark side of the desire for approval, however, is the fear of disapproval. Fear of being criticized or rejected by others is the most common reason people get detoured from the path God planned for them.

Our purpose is to please God, not people.
He alone examines the motives of our hearts.

1 THESSALONIANS 2:4 NLT

Why People-Pleasing Is Dangerous

- People-pleasing will cause you to miss God's will for your life.
- People-pleasing prevents your faith from growing.
- People-pleasing leads you to other sins.
- People-pleasing causes hypocrisy.
- People-pleasing silences your life message.

Jesus said to the Pharisees,

You are always making yourselves look good,
but God sees what is in your heart. The things
that most people think are important are worthless
as far as God is concerned.

LUKE 16:15 CEV

Break free from the fear of disapproval so you can enthusiastically
share the powerful message God wants to communicate through you!

Many even of the authorities did believe in him.
But they would not admit it for fear of the Pharisees,
in case they should be excommunicated.
They were more concerned to have the approval
of men than to have the approval of God.

JOHN 12:42–43 PHILLIPS

Do not follow the crowd in doing wrong.

EXODUS 23:2 NIV

You try to get praise from each other, but you
do not try to get the praise that comes from
the only God. So how can you believe?

JOHN 5:44 NCV

Truths to Help You Resist Peer Pressure

- Even God can't please everyone!
- You don't need anyone's approval to be happy.
- What seems so important now is only temporary.
- You only have to please one person!
- One day you will give an account of your life to God.

If the Son sets you free, you will be free indeed.
JOHN 8:36 NIV

*The world and everything in it that people desire
is passing away; but those who do the will
of God live forever.*
1 JOHN 2:17 GNT

Prayer: Dear God, one day you will ask if I fulfilled the purpose you created me for. With your help, I commit to live my life so that I can say I did not let anything distract me from that purpose!

Yes, each of us will give a personal account to God.
ROMANS 14:12 NLT

*No mere man has ever seen, heard,
or even imagined what wonderful things
God has ready for those who love the Lord.*
1 CORINTHIANS 2:9 TLB

This phrase is the ultimate definition of a life well-lived. You do the eternal and timeless (God's purpose) in a contemporary and timely way (in your generation). That is what the purpose-driven life is all about. Neither past nor future generations can serve God's purpose in this generation. Will you be a person God can use for his purpose? Will you serve God's purpose in your generation?

When fulfilling your purposes seems tough, don't give in to discouragement. Remember your reward, which will last forever.

I consider that our present sufferings are not worth comparing with the glory that will be revealed in us.

ROMANS 8:18 NIV

Look, I am coming soon! My reward is with me, and I will give to each person according to what they have done.

REVELATION 22:12 NIV

A PRAYER FOR YOUR PURPOSE

Father, more than anything else, I want to live for you and the five purposes that you created me to fulfill.

I want my life to bring you pleasure as I live a lifestyle of worship.

I want to be used to build the fellowship of your family, the church.

I want to become like Jesus in the way I think and feel and act.

I want to use the shape you've given me for a ministry to other believers in the Body of Christ.

I want to fulfill my mission in the world by telling others about your love. Help me to reach one more for Jesus. Help me to pass on the message of your purposes to others.

Dear Lord, I want to serve your purposes in my generation, so that one day I may hear you say, "Well done, good and faithful servant."

In Jesus' name, Amen.

SOURCES

Text compiled from: A sermon entitled "What on Earth Am I Here For?" by Pastor Rick Warren of Saddleback Church.

The Purpose Driven Life. By Rick Warren. © 2002 by Rick Warren. Grand Rapids, MI: Zondervan, 2002.

Scripture quotations marked CEV are taken from the Contemporary English Version. Copyright © 1991, 1992, 1995 by American Bible Society. Used by permission.

Scripture quotations marked NIV are taken from The Holy Bible, New International Version®, NIV®. Copyright © 1973, 1978, 1984, 2011 by Biblica, Inc.® Used by permission of Zondervan. All rights reserved worldwide. www.Zondervan.com. The "NIV" and "New International Version" are trademarks registered in the United States Patent and Trademark Office by Biblica, Inc.®

Scripture quotations marked ESV are taken from the ESV® Bible (The Holy Bible, English Standard Version®). Copyright © 2001 by Crossway, a publishing ministry of Good News Publishers. Used by permission. All rights reserved.

Scripture quotations marked GNT are taken from the Good News Translation® (Today's English Version, Second Edition). Copyright © 1992 American Bible Society. All rights reserved.

Scripture quotations marked GW are taken from *God's Word*®. Copyright © 1995 God's Word to the Nations. Used by permission of Baker Publishing Group. All rights reserved.

Scripture quotations marked KJV are taken from the King James Version. Public domain.

Scripture quotations marked TLB are taken from The Living Bible. Copyright © 1971. Used by permission of Tyndale House Publishers, Inc., Carol Stream, Illinois 60188. All rights reserved.

Scripture quotations marked The Message are taken from *THE MESSAGE.* Copyright © 1993, 2002, 2018 by Eugene H. Peterson. Used by permission of NavPress. All rights reserved. Represented by Tyndale House Publishers, Inc.

Scripture quotations marked NASB are taken from the New American Standard Bible®. Copyright © 1960, 1962, 1963, 1968, 1971, 1972, 1973, 1975, 1977, 1995 by The Lockman Foundation. Used by permission. (www.Lockman.org).

Scripture quotations marked NCV are taken from the New Century Version®. Copyright © 2005 by Thomas Nelson. Used by permission. All rights reserved.

Scripture quotations marked NJB are taken from *The New Jerusalem Bible.* Copyright © 1985 Darton, Longman & Todd, Ltd. and Doubleday, a division of Bantam Doubleday Dell Publishing Group, Inc., Garden City, NY.

Scripture quotations marked NLT are taken from the Holy Bible, New Living Translation. Copyright © 1996, 2004, 2015 by Tyndale House Foundation. Used by permission of Tyndale House Publishers, Inc., Carol Stream, Illinois 60188. All rights reserved.

Scripture quotations marked NRSV are taken from the New Revised Standard Version Bible. Copyright © 1989, Division of Christian Education of the National Council of the Churches of Christ in the United States of America. Used by permission. All rights reserved.

Scripture quotations marked PHILLIPS are taken from The New Testament in Modern English by J. B. Phillips. Copyright © 1960, 1972 J. B. Phillips. Administered by the Archbishops' Council of the Church of England. Used by permission.